YOUR KNOWLEDGE HAS VALUE

Gebhard Deißler

A Paris-Beijing International Strategic Alliance

An Intercultural Business Case Study Report

GRIN Verlag

Bibliografische Information der Deutschen Nationalbibliothek:

Die Deutsche Bibliothek verzeichnet diese Publikation in der Deutschen National-
bibliografie; detaillierte bibliografische Daten sind im Internet über http://dnb.d-
nb.de/ abrufbar.

Imprint:

Copyright © 2013 GRIN Verlag GmbH
Druck und Bindung: Books on Demand GmbH, Norderstedt Germany
ISBN: 978-3-656-56583-3

This book at GRIN:

http://www.grin.com/en/e-book/212910/a-paris-beijing-international-strategic-
alliance

GRIN - Your knowledge has value

Der GRIN Verlag publiziert seit 1998 wissenschaftliche Arbeiten von Studenten, Hochschullehrern und anderen Akademikern als eBook und gedrucktes Buch. Die Verlagswebsite www.grin.com ist die ideale Plattform zur Veröffentlichung von Hausarbeiten, Abschlussarbeiten, wissenschaftlichen Aufsätzen, Dissertationen und Fachbüchern.

Visit us on the internet:

http://www.grin.com/

http://www.facebook.com/grincom

http://www.twitter.com/grin_com

Transcultural Management

Gebhard Deißler D.E.A./UNIV. PARIS I

A
PARIS-BEIJING
INTERNATIONAL
STRATEGIC
ALLIANCE

AN INTERCULTURAL BUSINESS CASE STUDY REPORT

CULTURE   RESEARCH

KULTUR FORSCHUNG

RECHERCHE CULTURE

BÚSQUEDA CULTURAL

RICERCA   CULTURALE

跨文化的智慧精髓

Итранскультурная

Interkulturelles- u. Transkulturelles Management (German)

Intercultural &Transcultural Management (English)

Gestion Interculturelle et Gestion Transculturelle (French)

Gerencia Intercultural y Gerencia Transcultural (Spanish)

Gerência Intercultural e Gerência Transcultural (Portuguese)

跨文化的智慧精髓 - kua wen hua de zhi hui jing sui (Chinese)

транскультурная компетенция - transkulturnaja
kompetencija (Russian)

toransukaruchā　・ manējimento (Japanese)
トランスカルチャー　・　マネジメント

Vishua Chaytana (Sanskrit)

Index

CHINEFARGE

A SINO-WESTERN JOINT VENTURE

A CASE STUDY REPORT

1

The Business Case

'Chinefarge' is an intercultural business case study report and refers to a Sino-western joint venture of Paris-based LAFARGE and Huabei Mining Company (HMC) near Beijing. Lafarge is a major global player in building materials that tries to gain a foothold in Asia, more specifically in China which has an extraordinary need of construction materials and know-how to satisfy its emergent economy. While one can gain market share and the other a powerful partner, the cultural challenges of the IJV constituted a barrier for both sides. This succinct case study report diagnoses the cultural challenges they encountered in the initial stages of the joint venture and recommends some solutions.

This case study report was an assignment within the context of an Advanced Intercultural Management Programme of the University of Cambridge in the United Kingdom and was completed according to stipulated conditions in a precisely limited number of words, in 2004.

2

Culture Profiles (Societal and Organisational) of Joint Venture Partners

Dimensions of cultural difference	Partnering cultures' values	
	France	China
1. Context	Mid-range	High
2. Individualism/Collectivism (IDV)		
3. Power distance (PDI)	67	80
4. Masculinity (MAS/FEM)	46	50
5. Uncertainty Avoidance (UAI)	83	46
6. Long-term Orientation (LTO)	Medium term	118 Long-term
7. Individualism-Communitarianism	Communitarian	Communitarian
8. Specificity versus Diffuseness	Specific	Diffuse
9. Universalism versus Particularism	Universalist	Particularist
10. Neutral versus Affective/Emotional	Emotional	Emotional

11. Achievement versus Ascription	Ascription	Ascription
12. Inner directed versus Outer directed	Outer -/Coach government	Highly outer dir.
13. Space conception	Private/close	Public/close
14. Time conception (sequential/synchronouos)	Synchronous	Synchronous
15. Org.: Task versus social system	36 sys (imp. social group)	67 system
16. Face	Personal integrity	Group integrity
17. Personal connections	Elite	Guanxi
18. Harmony		Wa/he
19. Trust	Higher trust	Lower trust
20. Gender	Gender equality	Male preference
21. Humaneness	Unsp. humane	Unspecified
22. Decision making	Negotiator empowerment	Consensus
23. Negotiation style/strategy	Non-zero sum game	zero sum
24. Emergent organisational cultural profile	Full bureaucracy/pyramid of people	Tribe/Family
25. Preferred coordination mechanism	Standardization of work processes	Direct supervision
26. Key part of the organization	Technostructure	Strategic apex
27. Authority	Person and rules-vested authority	Person-vested authority
28. Conflict behavior	Acceptance	Avoidance
29. Thinking style	Deductive	Holistic, big picture; moving in spiral, generating

		holistic image centered on a general line of thought
30. Interpersonal speaking distance	Smaller than China	Bigger than West
31. East-West Management Dichotomy	Rationality	Relationships
	Structured	Flexible
	Directive	Adaptive
	Doing	Being

CHINEFARGE: A SINO - WESTERN JOINT VENTURE.

A CONCISE CASE STUDY REPORT

Culture: Corporate asset or liability?

Due to the high concentration of dysfunctionalities in the psychological area, signaling insufficient cultural awareness by JV partners, I raise the question: What can be done to make culture work for, instead of against the JV, in line with Ghoshal's, Bartlett's and Birkinshaw's emerging change management model (2002, p374), which addresses first psychology, then physiology and finally anatomy?

Attitudes

Identification with the organization

Attitudinal, behavioral and relational deficits seem to be imputable to the impossibility of reciprocating obedience and loyalty for care and control. The parent company, high on IDV, might have underestimated the vertical collectivist core values. It must evidence that the principle of reciprocation is complied with, to obtain the trade-off of identification, trust, discipline etc. Additionally, it depends on the solution of the double loyalty problem, discussed below. It can also be fostered through facework (mianzi) in the sense that affiliation with a notable global corporation is by itself face-giving to the Chinese. Additionally, in a vertical collectivist society, which differentiates between 'in-group' and 'out-group', it can be promoted by using 'renqing' (technique of converting out-group in in-group) and guanxi (doing mutual favors in the interest of long-lasting family of friendship-based relations) (Smith and Peterson, 2002, p.230). All in all, JV strategic policy should be aware of and accept Confucian/Taoist cultural standards, first and foremost 'He' (harmony, equality in inequality) along with Danwei, which together constitute the all pervasive reciprocity principle, based on the high PDI, collectivist (vertical -) orientation. Those standards being not met, even low UAV Chinese experience strong anxiety. Thus, the need of not only accepting, but reconciling core values as JV corporate success factors.

Relationships

Loyalty - Individualism/Collectivism - Time-Orientation

Whereas western individualism identifies with the JV, the collectivist orientation implies not only identification with the company but extends the reference group to society at large. The benefits of the JV with its limited life cycle and the long-term benefits of the macro-system are interconnected, which raises the issue of conflicting loyalties towards the Joint Venture, the former HMC danwei and the country at large. Absence of identification with the JV and competing loyalties form a vicious circle. It may be transformed into a virtuous circle through trust building.

Evolution of Trust

The evolution of trust can be effected, according to Blomquist's model of operationalising trust, through moral responsibility and positive intentions or, according to Johnson, J and Cullen, J B (2002, p.342) on the following three bases of trust: 'motivational investment, risk and interdependence'. Through the lens of Bennets IDM model transposed to the interfacing of organizational cultures, the employees are still at the ethnocentric stage.

Trust and Collectivism

Research evidence suggests that collectivism and general trust correlate negatively. Collectivism needs more specific referents for the evolution of trust. Hence, to underpin communication policy, trust building and trade-offs need specific referents and substantiation by concrete measures. HSE/HR are areas for implementing specific measures with high visibility.

Structures

Organizational Models

Host country and parent company organizational models (Hofstede 1980, p. 316) coincide in person-vested authority. The parent company also leads by rules-based authority and empowers middle management. Lack of management education, impairment of mianzi and guanxi resist the alignment. Supporting cultural standards are: The vertical collectivist society considers 'hierarchy as a given' Triandis, 2002, p. 25.) Adding a new echelon of real power fulfills the Confucian precepts according to which 'he' reins, when everybody is in the right place and in the right role. It is also culturally enforceable by the high PDI strategic apex.

The Board

Cultural polarizations within conflict with the parent organizational culture of unity of command and strategic apex of the host country organizational culture. Evidence of language and culture barriers should best be addressed by culture-specific intercultural training/coaching. A disunited board cannot serve as a role model of masterly charisma leading by vision and example of cultural integration. It must be a beacon of integration and communicate this vision internally and externally. Intercultural leadership differences in communicating visions should be considered. The Chinese mode of quiet politicking is what this culture is responsive to. Culturally rebalancing the composition of the board progressively would offset the deincentivizing polarization with the 'foreigners'.

HSE, Accommodation

Management can leverage the principle of reciprocation and specifically substantiate communication strategy by enhancing these areas - upgrading HSE-infrastructure, systems and services by EU parent company standards - in a visible way as a trade-off for higher standards in rules compliance and performance behavior. 'Managers from diffuse cultures communicate their respect by showing concern for an employee's whole life' (Adler 2003, p.48).

HR, Communications

Internal Communications and Training

Joint capabilities of awareness-building, information and training must be employed to adapt the skill-set and mindset of managers, who in turn channel the changes to the subordinates. Autocratic top management, deferent middle management and obedient employees face the dilemma that they have to trade centuries old role behaviours against a participative management paradigm; open, direct communication, individualistic, task- and performance oriented, highly polarized with the local cultural standards. Having learnt the US lesson regarding transferability, one should rather involve the target organizational culture in the shaping of an evolutionary localization process.

Strategic relationships management at board level and organizational culture change management need to synergize to enhance image, recruitment, retention and processes.

Strategic communications

Success of Chinefarge depends on how its internal and external interfacing issues are solved. Needing training and knowledge support by Lafarge S.A., Paris, ongoing communication, information flows and personnel rotation need enhancing. Due to the collectivist interconnectedness of Chinefarge with the macro-system, it is essential to develop communications and relationships with the key stakeholders (government, party, unions, community, [schools, hospitals]) through formal and informal communication, sponsoring and event management; highly visible, specific trust-building factors.

Performance management systems

Competitive entrepreneurial spirit seems to be deeper-rooted than conditioned egalitarianism. Research evidence testifies: 'the Chinese were likely to seek both success and failure feedback' (Audia and Tams, 2002, p.147) and a preference for 'equity over equality based reward' (Steer and Sanchez-Runde, 2002, p.206). A more competitive market economy, high scores on achievement orientation, LTO and strong verticality support them.

Performance: LTO - Speed and Quality

LTO involves a different notion of speed. The notion of quality seems to be situation-, relationship- and task-contingent. This complex is highly polarized with the foreign partner's shorter- term, higher speed and normed quality business culture. It requires evolutionary cultural engineering.

Conclusion

Due to the priority of culture an evolutionary approach to change management is preferable. Culture is no obstacle to the introduction of cutting-edge technology

14

and management. It can be an enhancing factor if properly leveraged.

Literature

Adler, N (2002) *International Dimensions of Organizational Behavior*, South-Western, Cincinnati, Oh. ISBN: 0-324-05786-5

Apfelthaler, G (2002) *Interkulturelles Management: Die Bewältigung interkultureller Differenzen in der internationalen Unternehmenstätigkeit.* Manz, Wien

Audia, PG and Tams, S (2002) 'Goal Setting, Performance Appraisal, Feedback' in Gannon, M J and Newman, L (Eds.) *The Blackwell Handbook of Cross-Cultural Management*, Blackwell Publishers, Oxford. ISBN: 0-631-21430-5

Bartlett, CH and Ghoshal, S and Birkinshaw (2003) *Transnational Management. Text, Cases, and Readings in Cross-Border Management*, International Edition, McGraw-Hill/Irwine, New York, NY. ISBN: 007-123228-1

Belbin (1996) *Team Roles at Work.* Butterworth-Heinemann

Bond (1988) *The Cross-Cultural Challenge to Social Psychology.* Books on Demand.

Brannen MY and Salk JE (2000) Partnering Across Borders: Negotiating organizational culture in a German-Japanese joint venture, *Human Relations*, Volume 53(4) 451-487, Sage Publications, London

Brosse, T (1984). *La Conscience-Energie. Structure de l'Homme et de l'Univers. Ses implications scientifiques, sociales et spirituelles.* Editions Présence. Sisteron.

ISBN 2-901696-15-5

Davison, S C, Ward K (1999) *Leading International Teams*. McGraw-Hill. Maidenhead.
ISBN: 0 07 709209 4.

Delahaye, Y (1977) *La Frontière Et Le Texte*, Payot, Paris. ISBN: 2-228-11850-09
Ewington, N (2004) *Workbook Unit 1, Workbook unit 2 and Workbook Unit 3*,
CPI University of Cambridge, UK

Ghemawat, P (2001) Distance Still Matters. The Hard Reality of Global Expansion.
Harvard Business Review. September 2001

Goodall, K and Roberts, J (2003) Repairing Managerial Knowledge-Ability over
Distance. Organisation Studies 24 (7): 1153 – 1175, Sage Publications, London

Goodall, K and Roberts, J (2003) Only connect: teamwork in the multinational.
Journal of World Business 38 (2003) 150-164, Pergamon

Goodall, K (2002) Managing to Learn: from cross-cultural theory to education
practice, Warner M and Joynt P (Eds.) *Managing Across Cultures: Issues and
Perspectives*. Thompson Learning

Govindarajan, V and Gupta A K (2001) Building an Effective Global Business Team,
MIT Sloan Management Review, Summer 2001

Hampden-Turner, Ch and *Trompenaars*, F (2002) *Building Cross-Cultural Competence.
How to create wealth from conflicting values,* John Wiley and Sons Ltd,
Chichester, England. ISBN: 0-471-49527-1

Hall, E (1990) *Beyond Culture.* Anchor

Hersey, P and Blanchard, K H (1993) *Management of Organizational Behaviour:
Utilizing Human Resources, 6th edition,* Prentice Hall

Hickson, DJ and Pugh, DS (2001) *Management Worldwide. Distinctive Styles Amid
Globalization,* Penguin Books Ltd, London. ISBN: 0-14100603-X

Hodgetts, R M and Luthans, F (2003): *International Management: culture, strategy, and
behaviour,* Boston, Mass., McGraw-Hill

Hofstede, G (1980) *Culture's Consequences, International Differences in Work-Related
Values,* Sage Publications, Newbury Park, Ca. ISBN: 0-8039-1444-

Hofstede, G (2002) *Cultures and Organizations. Intercultural Cooperation and its*

Importance for Survival. Software of the Mind, Profile Books Ltd, London. ISBN: 1-86197-543-Hofstede, G (2003) *Culture and Organizations. Intercultural Cooperation and itsImportance for Survival, Software of the Mind, Profile Books Ltd, London.* ISBN: 1 8697 543 0

Hofstede, G and Hofstede, G J (2005) *Culture and Organizations. Intercultural Cooperation and its Importance for Survival, Software of the Mind,* McGraw-Hill: ISBN: 0-07-143959-5

Holden, N (2004) *German as a Language of Management: Pragmatic Observations of German-style Networking and Knowledge-Sharing,* Interknow Workshop II, Regensburg.

Knapp, K (1996) 'Interpersonale und interkulturelle Kommunikation' in Bergemann, N (Ed.) *Interkulturelle Kommunikation,* Physica-Verlag, Heidelberg. ISBN: 3-7908-0913-6

Maisonrouge J (1988) *Inside IBM. A European's Story.* Collins. London. ISBN: 0-00-217692-0

Mole, J (1993) *Mind your Manners. Managing Culture Clash in the Single European Market,* Industrial Society Press, London. ISBN: 1 85788 000 5

Mullins, L J (2002) *Management and Organisational Behaviour, 6th edition,* Prentice Hall

Naipaul V S. (1984) *Finding the Centre,* Penguin Books Ltd. Harmondsworth, Middlesex, England

Price, S (2000) 'A View from a Bridge: Stereotypes of the German in Business and Higher Education' in Emig, R (Ed.) Stereotypes in Contemporary Anglo-German Relations', Macmillan Press Ltd, Basingstoke. ISBN: 0-333-79341-2

Steers, R and Sanchez-Runde, C (2002) 'Culture, Motivation, and Work Bahavior' in Gannon, M J and Newman, K L (Eds.) *The Blackwell Handbook of Cross-Cultural Management, Blackwell Publishers,* Oxford. ISBN: 0-631-21430-5

Stuart, R and Barsoux, JL and Kieser, A and Ganter, HD and Wagenbach, P (1994) *Managing in Britain and in Germany,* The Macmillan Press Ltd, Basingstoke. ISBN: 0-312-12237-3

Triandis, H C (2002) 'Generic Individualism and Collectivism' in Gannon, M J and Newman, KL (Eds.) *The Blackwell Handbook of Cross-Cultural Management,* Blackwell Publishers Ltd, Oxford. ISBN: 0-631-21430-5

Weidenfeld, G (1999) "Englisches Deutschlandbild" in *Die Politische Meinung,* Volume 358, Nr.10, pp 55-62. ISSN: 00323446.

Yong, L and Kammhuber, S (2003) 'Ostasien: China' (East-Asia: China) in Thomas, A and Kinast, U and Schroll-Machl, S (Eds.) *Handbuch der Internationalen Kommunikation und Kooperation, Band 1. (Handbook of International Communication and Cooperation, Volume 1)* Vandenhoeck & Ruprecht, Goettingen. ISBN: 3-525-46172-0.

Worldwork (2002) *International Management Development. The International Profiler,* London: